Progressive
GUITAR METHOD

Book 1:
Supplement

by
Gary Turner

Visit our Website
www.learntoplaymusic.com

The Progressive Series of Music Instruction Books, CDs, and DVDs

2

CONTENTS

CONTENTS CONT.

INTRODUCTION

THE PROGRESSIVE GUITAR METHOD is a series of books designed to take the Guitar student from a beginner level through to a professional standard of playing. All books are carefully graded, lesson by lesson methods which assume no prior knowledge on your behalf. Within the series all styles and techniques of guitar playing are covered, including reading music, playing chords and rhythms, lead guitar and fingerpicking.

PROGRESSIVE GUITAR METHOD BOOK 1: SUPPLEMENT is designed to be used in conjunction with Progressive Guitar Method Book 1: Beginner and contains an extra 70 songs to play, and 8 more lessons including information on major scales, keys, triplets, $\frac{6}{8}$ time, sixteenth notes, syncopation and swing rhythms. All guitarists should know all of the information in this book.
In conjunction with this book you can use other books in the progressive series to learn about tablature reading, lead guitar playing, fingerpicking, bar chords, slide and classical guitar styles as well as music theory and different styles such as Rock, Blues, Country, Jazz, Metal and Funk.

The best and fastest way to learn is to use these books in conjunction with:
1.   Buying sheet music and song books of your favourite recording artists and learning to play their songs.
2.   Practicing and playing with other musicians. You will be surprised how good a basic drums/bass/guitar combination can sound even when playing easy music.
3.   Learning by listening to your favourite CDs.

Also in the early stages it is helpful to have the guidance of an experienced teacher. This will also help you keep to a schedule and obtain weekly goals.

Guitar Method
Book 1

A comprehensive, lesson by lesson introduction to the guitar, covering notes on all 6 strings, reading music, picking technique, basic music theory and incorporating well known traditional pop/rock, folk and blues songs.

Guitar Method
Rhythm

Introduces all the important open chord shapes for major, minor, seventh, sixth, major seventh, minor seventh, suspended, diminished and augmented chords. Learn to play over 50 chord progressions, including 12 Bar Blues and Turnaround progressions.

Guitar Method
Lead

Covers scales and patterns over the entire fretboard so that you can improvise against major, minor, and Blues progressions in any key. Learn the licks and techniques used by all lead guitarists such as hammer-ons, slides, bending, vibrato, and more.

Guitar Method
Fingerpicking

Introduces right hand fingerpicking patterns that can be used as an accompaniment to any chord, chord progression or song. Covers alternate thumb, arpeggio and constant bass style as used in Rock, Pop, Folk, Country, Blues Ragtime and Classical music.

Guitar Method
Chords

Contains the most useful open, Bar and Jazz chord shapes of the most used chord types with chord progressions to practice and play along with. Includes sections on tuning, how to read sheet music, transposing, as well as an easy chord table, formula and symbol chart.

Guitar Method
Bar Chords

Introduces the most useful Bar, Rock and Jazz chord shapes used by all Rock/Pop/Country and Blues guitarist. Includes major, minor, seventh, sixth, major seventh, etc. Suggested rhythm patterns including percussive strums, dampening and others are also covered.

Guitar Method
Book 2

A comprehensive, lesson by lesson method covering the most important keys and scales for guitar, with special emphasis on bass note picking, bass note runs, hammer-ons etc. Featuring chordal arrangements of well known Rock, Blues, Folk and Traditional songs.

Guitar Method
Theory Book 1

A comprehensive, introduction to music theory as it applies to the guitar. Covers reading traditional music, rhythm notation and tablature, along with learning the notes on the fretboard, how to construct chords and scales, transposition, musical terms and playing in all keys.

For more information about the *Progressive Guitar Method* series as well as the general *Progressive* series, contact:

LTP Publishing
email: info@learntoplaymusic.com
or visit our website;
www.learntoplaymusic.com

APPROACH TO PRACTICE

It is important to have a correct approach to practice. You will benefit more from several short practices (e.g. 15-30 minutes per day) than one or two long sessions per week. This is especially so in the early stages, because of the basic nature of the material being studied. In a practice session you should divide your time evenly between the study of new material and the revision of past work. It is a common mistake for semi-advanced students to practice only the pieces they can already play well. Although this is more enjoyable, it is not a very satisfactory method of practice. You should also try to correct mistakes and experiment with new ideas. It is the author's belief that an experienced teacher will be an invaluable aid to your progress.

THE RUDIMENTS OF MUSIC

The musical alphabet consists of 7 letters: **A   B   C   D   E   F   G**

Music is written on a **staff**, which consists of 5 parallel lines between which there are 4 spaces.

MUSIC STAFF

The treble or 'G' clef is placed at the beginning of each staff line.

Treble or 'G' Clef ⟶

This clef indicates the position of the note G. (It is an old fashioned method of writing the letter G, with the centre of the clef being written on the second staff line.)

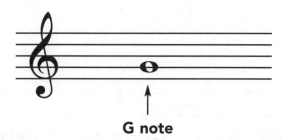

G note

The other lines and spaces on the staff are named as such:

Extra notes can be added by the use of short lines, called **leger lines**.

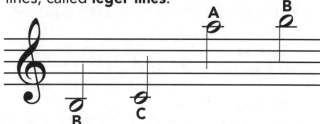

When a note is placed on the staff its head indicates its position, e.g.:

This is a G note   **This is a C note**

When the note head is below the middle staff line the stem points upward and when the head is above the middle line the stem points downward. A note placed on the middle line (**B**) can have its stem pointing either up or down.

Bar lines are drawn across the staff, which divides the music into sections called **bars** or **measures**. A **double bar line** signifies either the end of the music, or the end of an important section of it.

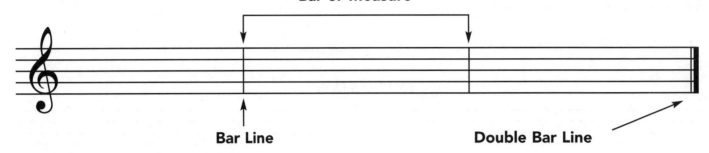

NOTE VALUES

The table below sets out the most common notes used in music and their respective time values (i.e. length of time held). For each note value there is an equivalent rest, which indicates a period of silence.

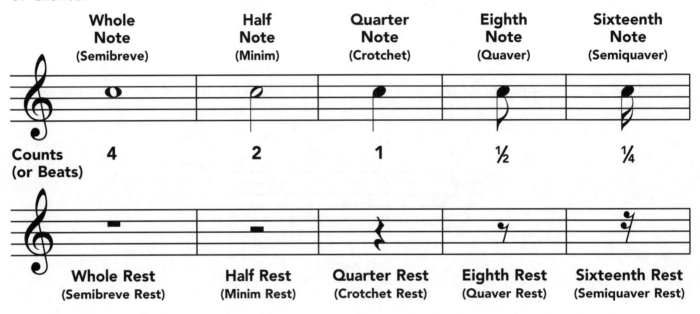

If a **dot** is placed after a note it increases the value of that note by half, e.g.

Dotted Half Note ♩• (2 + 1) = 3 counts

Dotted Eighth Note ♪. (½ + ¼) = ¾ counts

Dotted Quarter Note ♩• (1 + ½) = 1½ counts

Dotted Whole Note o• (4 + 2) = 6 counts

A **tie** is a curved line joining two or more notes of the same pitch, where the second note(s) **is note played** but its time value is added to that of the first note. Here are two examples:

In both of these examples only the first note is played.

TIME SIGNATURES

At the beginning of each piece of music, after the treble clef, is the **time signature**.

$\frac{4}{4}$ **Time Signature** (pronounced Four Four time)

The time signature indicates the number of beats per bar (the top number) and the type of note receiving one beat (the bottom number). For example:

4 – this indicates 4 beats per bar.

4 – this indicates that each beat is worth a quarter note (crotchet).

Thus in $\frac{4}{4}$ time there must be the equivalent of 4 quarter note beats per bar, e.g.

$\frac{4}{4}$ is the most common time signature and is sometimes represented by this symbol called **common time**.

Common Time

The other time signatures used in this book are;

Three Four Time
3 indicates three quarter
4 note beats per bar.

Two Four Time
2 indicates two quarter
4 note beats per bar.

Six Eight Time
6 indicates six eighth
8 note beats per bar.

USING THE COMPACT DISC

It is recommended that you have a copy of the accompanying compact disc that includes all the examples in this book. The book shows you where to put your fingers and what technique to use and the recording lets you hear how each example should sound. Practice the examples slowly at first, gradually increasing tempo. Once you are confident you can play the example evenly without stopping the beat, try playing along with the recording. You will hear a drum beat at the beginning of each example, to lead you into the example and to help you keep time. To play along with the CD your guitar must be in tune with it. If you have tuned using an electronic tuner (see next page) your guitar will already be in tune with the CD. A small diagram of a compact disc with a number as shown below indicates a recorded example. If you do not know how to tune your guitar see *Progressive Guitar Method Book 1: Beginner.*

 12 ⟵ **CD Track Number**

TUNING YOUR GUITAR TO THE CD

Before you commence each lesson or practice session you will need to tune your guitar. If your guitar is out of tune everything you play will sound incorrect even though you are holding the correct notes. On the accompanying CD the **first six tracks** correspond to the **six strings of the guitar**.

 1 **6th String**
E Note (Thickest string)

 2 **5th String**
A Note

3 **4th String**
D Note

4 **3rd String**
G Note

 5 **2nd String**
B Note

 6 **1st String**
E Note (Thinnest string)

7 Merrily

8 Lightly Row

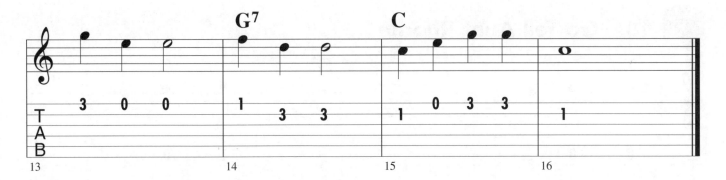

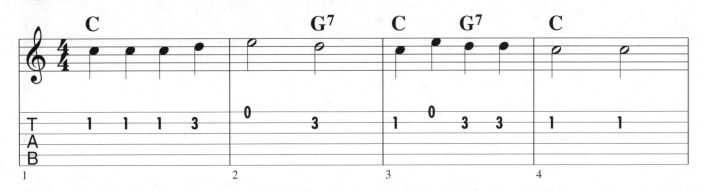

9 In the Light of the Moon

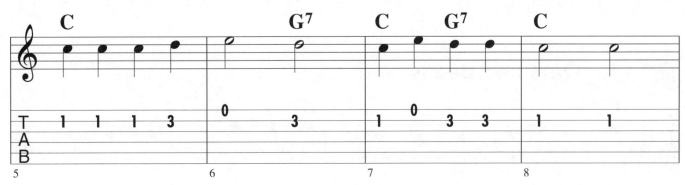

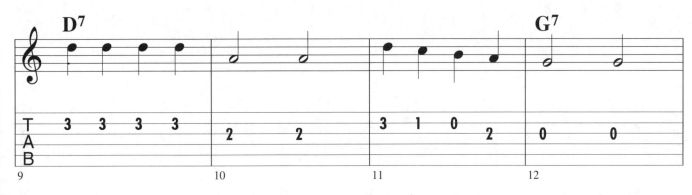

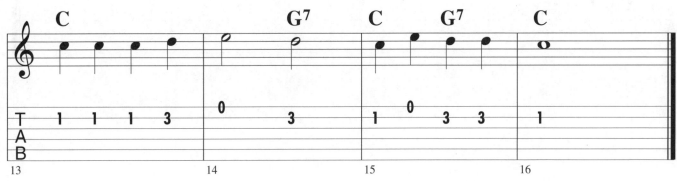

10 Go Tell Aunt Rhodie

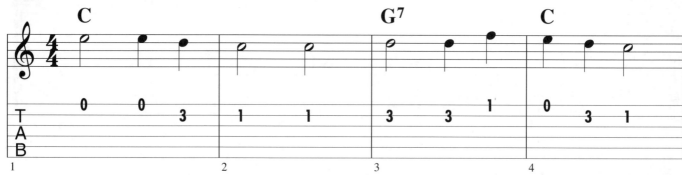

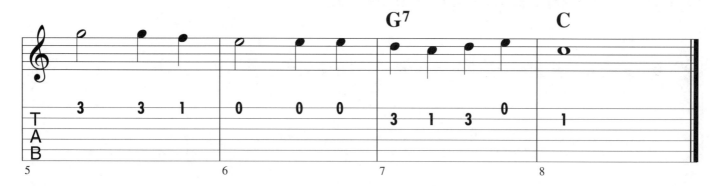

11 Oats and Beans

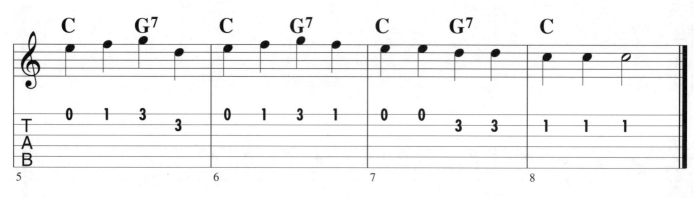

12 Twinkle Twinkle Little Star

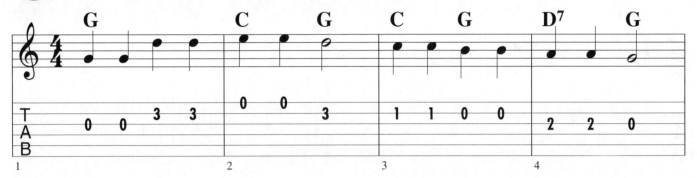

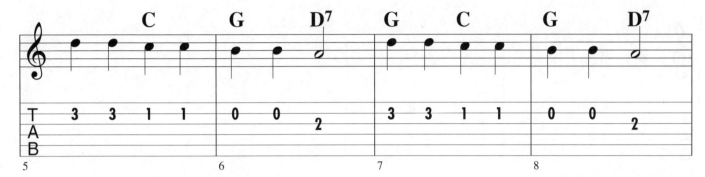

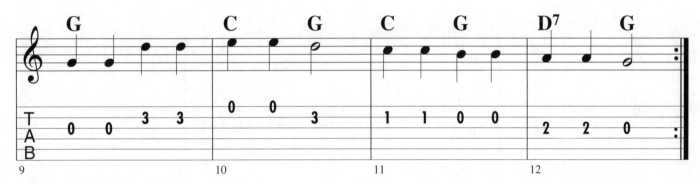

13 Yankee Doodle

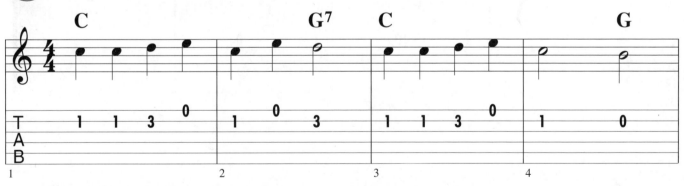

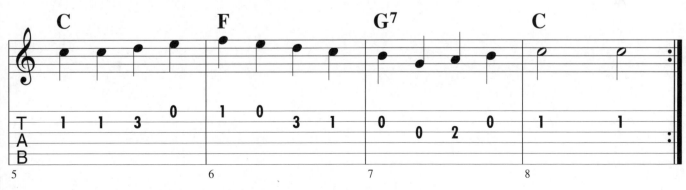

14 Strike Up the Band

15 Amazing Grace

14

 16 **When Johnny Comes Marching Home**

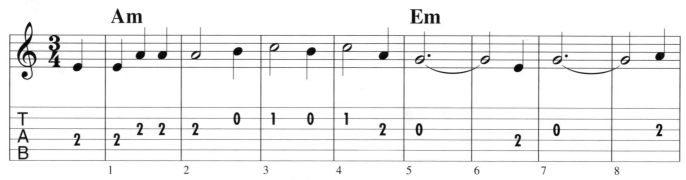

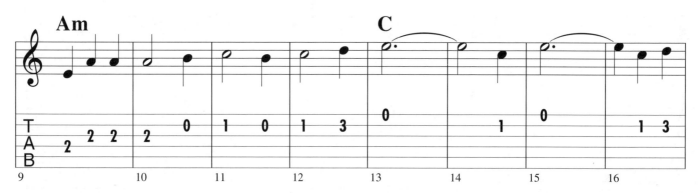

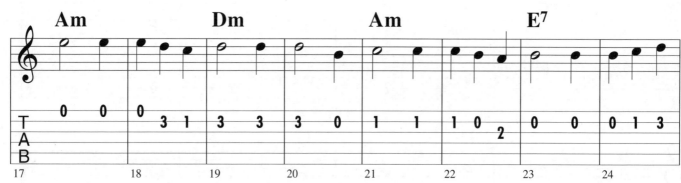

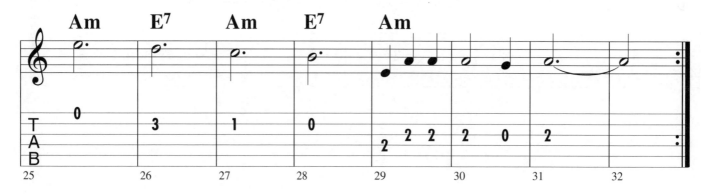

17 **Morning Has Broken**

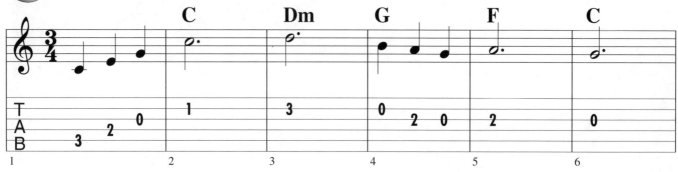

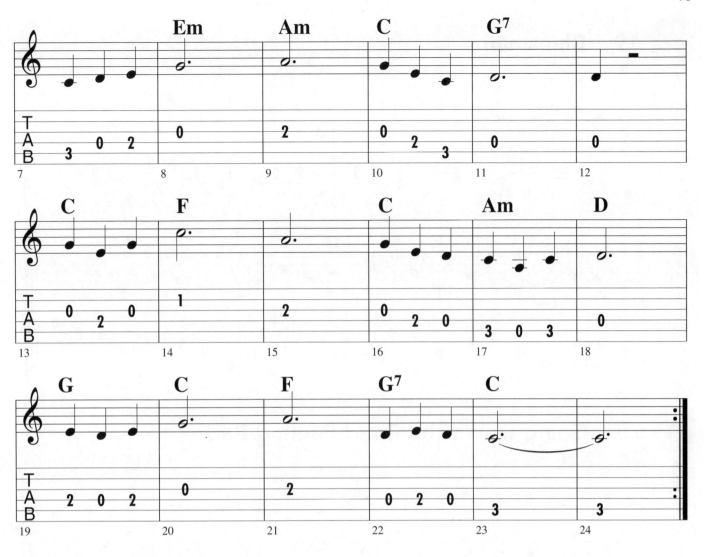

18   Minor Blues

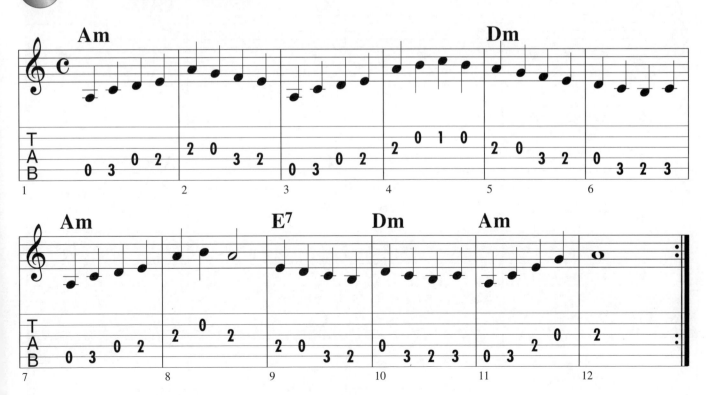

16

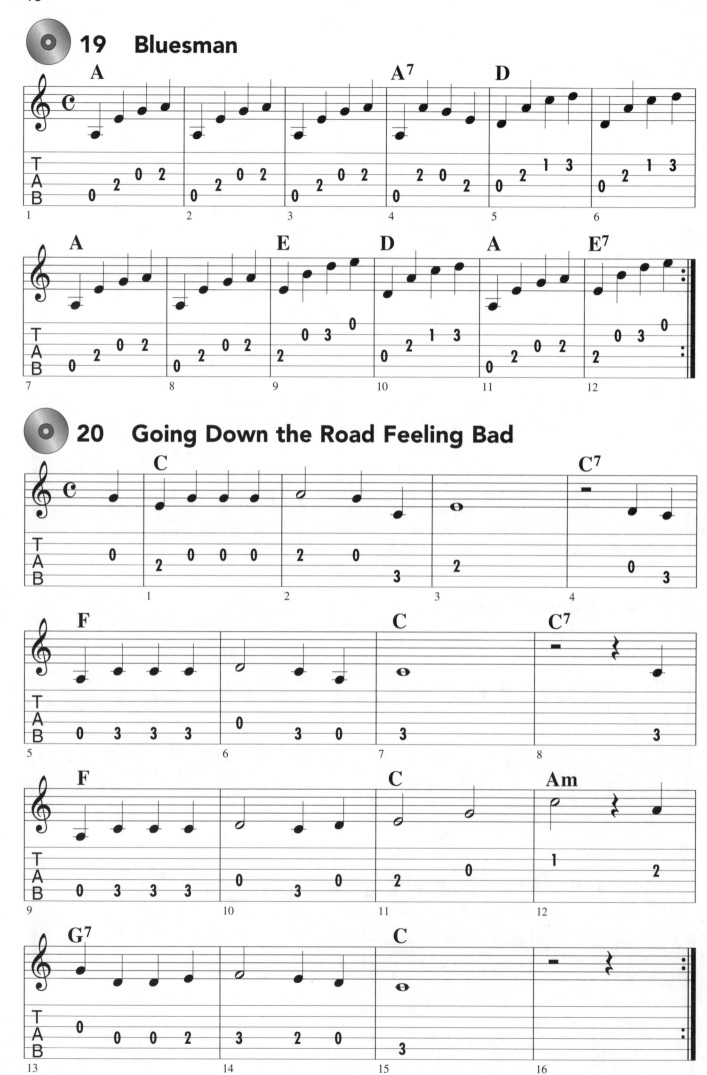

19 Bluesman

20 Going Down the Road Feeling Bad

21 Custer's Theme

18

 **22   Cool Blues**

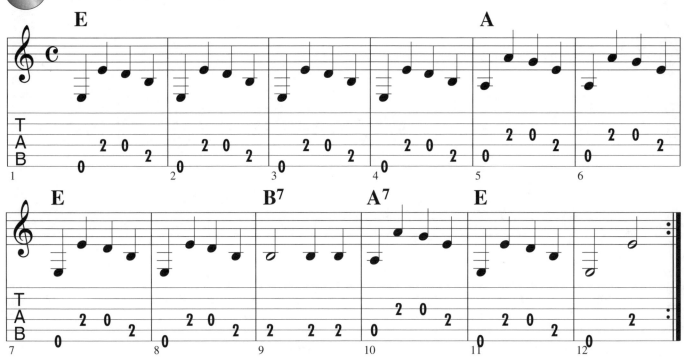

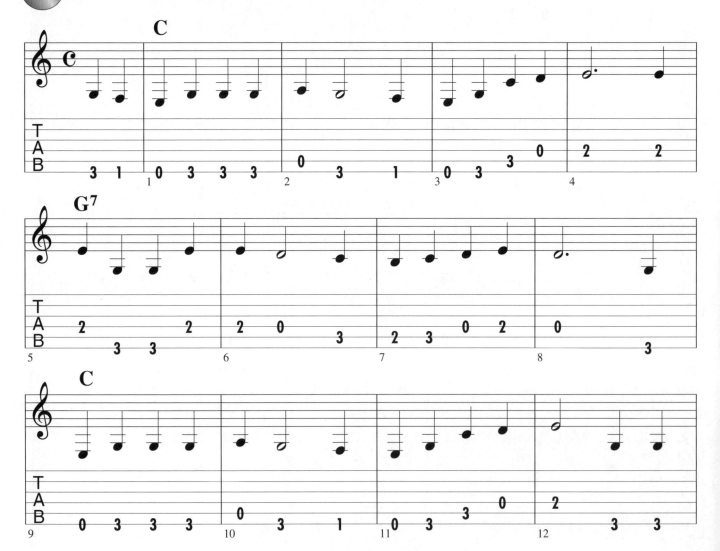

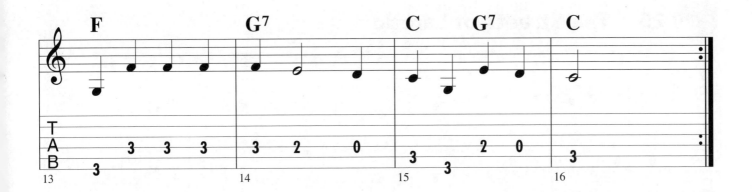

24 A Bicycle Built For Two

25   The Streets of Laredo

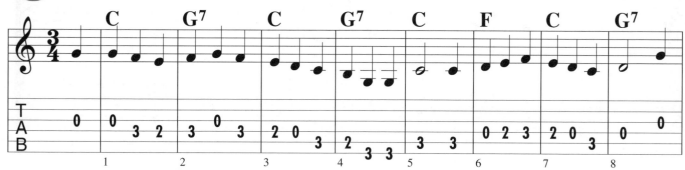

26   Red River Valley

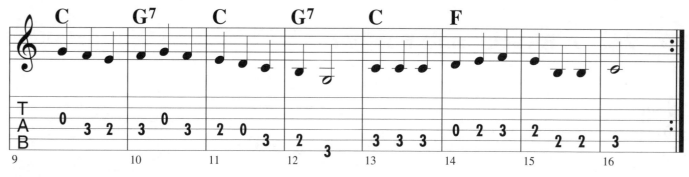

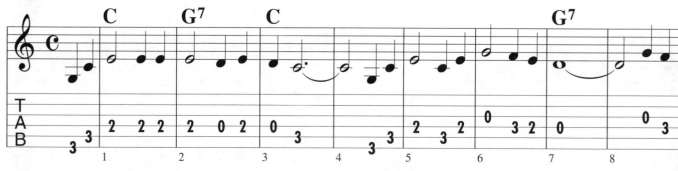

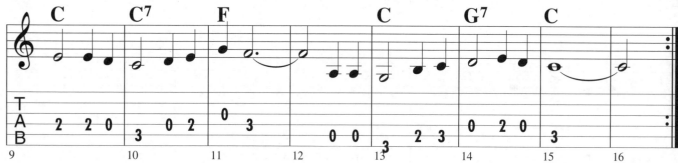

27   Hush Little Baby

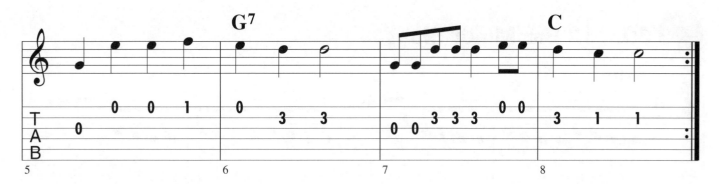

28 Pick a Bale o' Cotton

29 Shortin' Bread

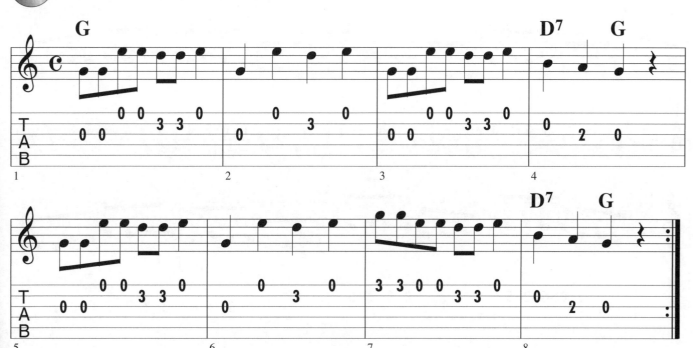

30   12 Bar Minor Blues

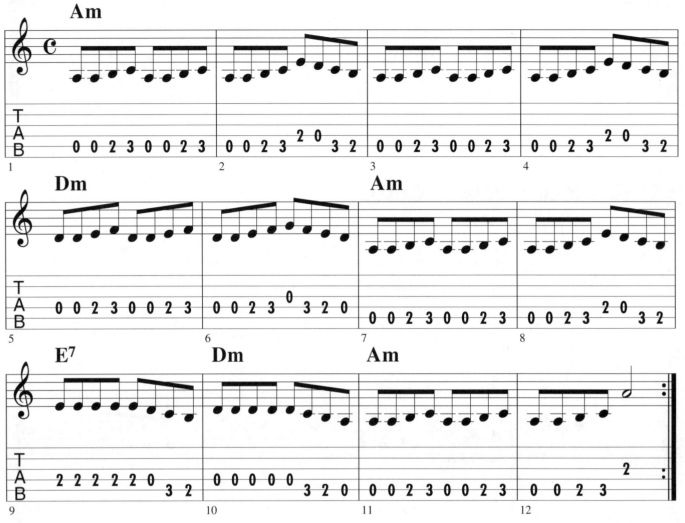

31   Rockabilly Blues

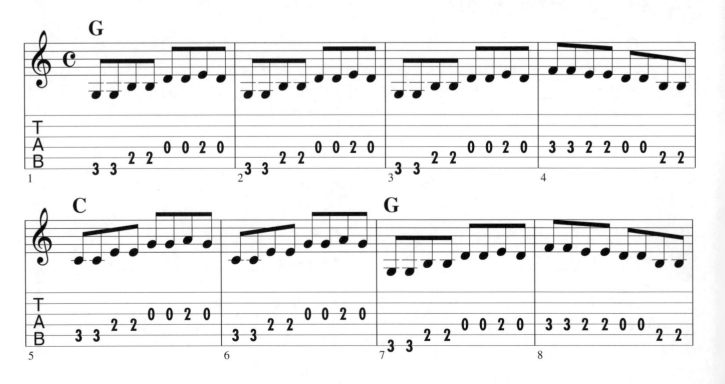

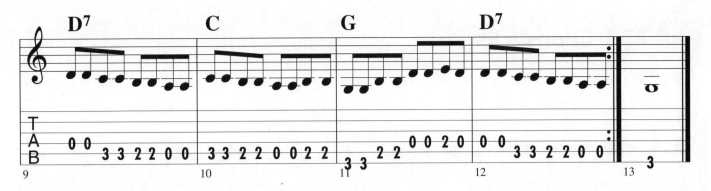

32   Dance of the Hours

33 **Chopsticks**

D.C. al Fine indicates that the song should be repeated from the beginning until the word fine (bar 16).

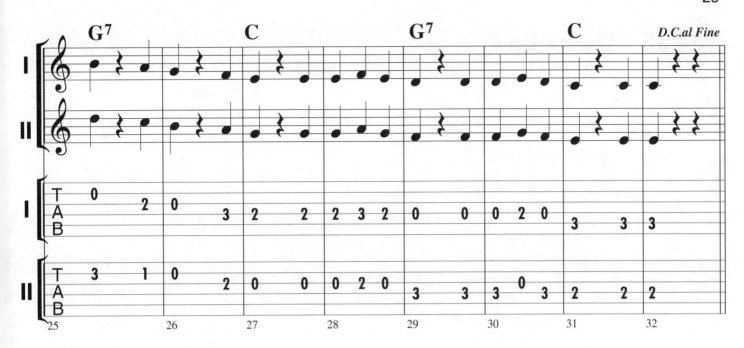

D.C.al Fine

 34 Shenandoah

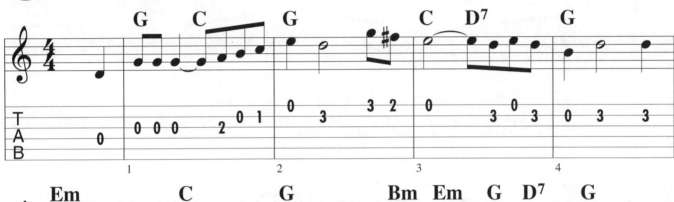

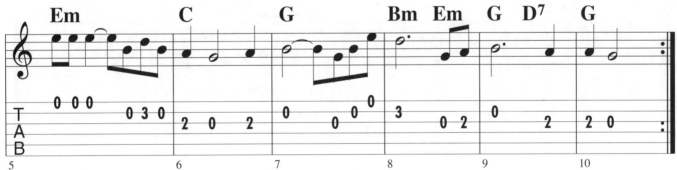

EIGHTH NOTE REST

This symbol is an eighth note rest. It indicates half a beat of silence.

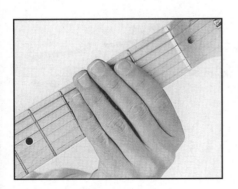

When a rest comes after you have played a note, you must stop the note sounding: ie, stop the strings vibrating (muting them). This can be achieved by placing your left hand fingers lightly on the strings. Do not press too hard as this will produce a new note. When using the left hand to mute a note, place the fingers flat over all six strings as this is easier than just muting one string. This muting technique is also useful to stop previously played notes sounding at the same time a new note is played. The following song 'Danny Boy' features the eighth note rest.

26

35 **Danny Boy**

36 **Rockin' Blues**

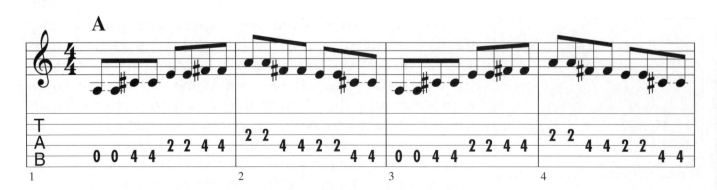

37   O Sole Mio

38 Take Me Out to the Ball Game

39 Hello My Baby

40 **Natural Blues**

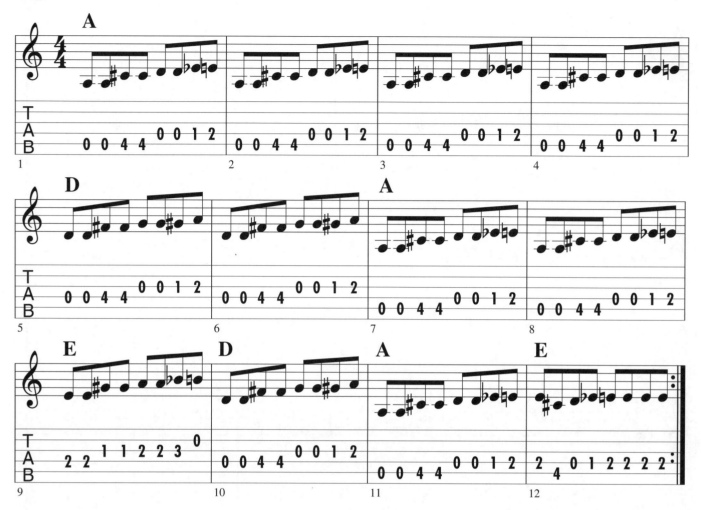

 41 **8 Bar Blues in the Key of C**

42 I Yi Yi Yi (Cielito Lindo)

43 La Spagnola

44 Habanera

45 Mussi Den

46 Swing Low, Sweet Chariot

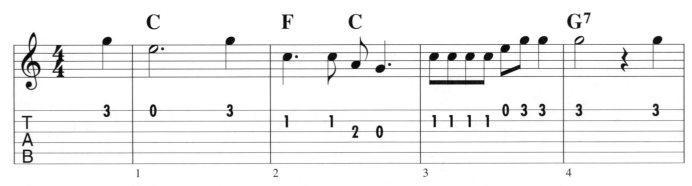

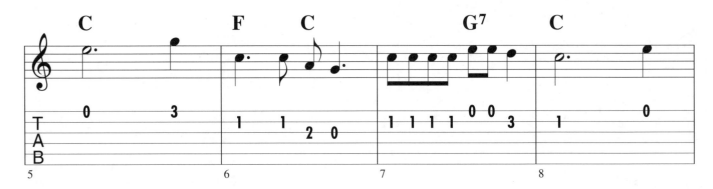

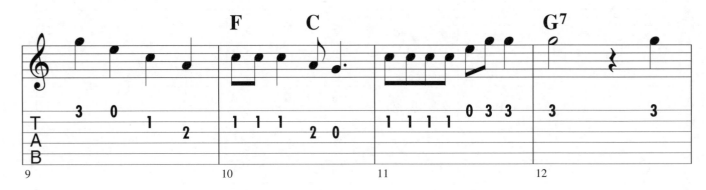

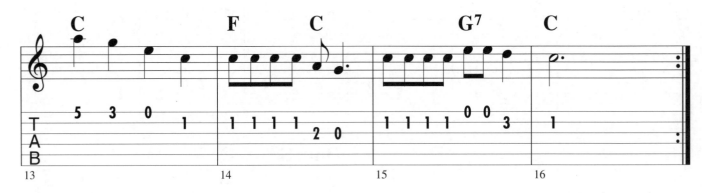

47 Fur Elise

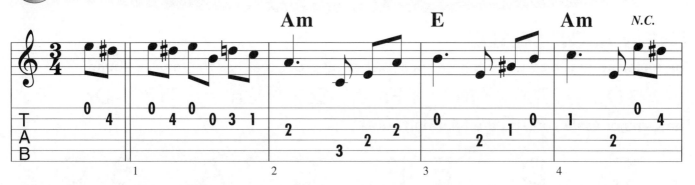

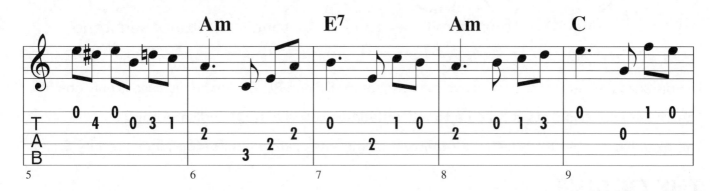

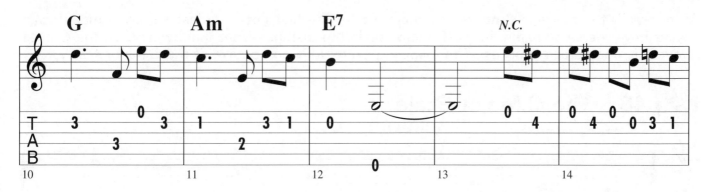

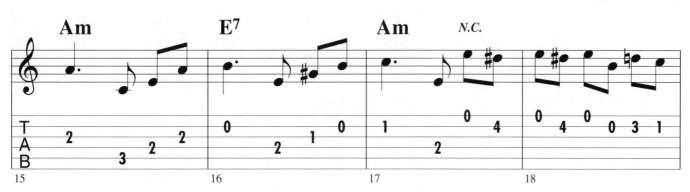

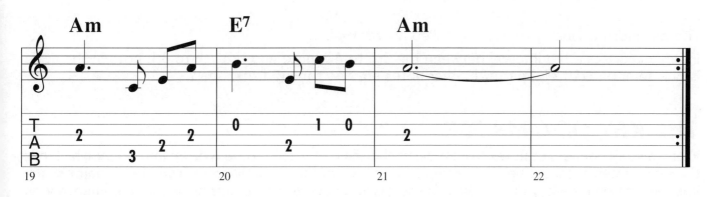

LESSON ELEVEN

THE MAJOR SCALE

The **major scale** is a series of **8** notes in alphabetical order that has the familiar sound:

Do   Re   Mi   Fa   So   La   Ti   Do

The **C major scale** contains the following notes.

C   D   E F   G   A   B C

tone	tone	semitone	tone	tone	tone	semitone
T	**T**	**ST**	**T**	**T**	**T**	**ST**

The distance between each note is two frets except for **EF** and **BC** where the distance is only one fret.

The distance of two frets is called a **tone** (sometimes called a **step**), indicated by **T**.

The distance of one fret is called a **semitone** (sometimes called a **half step**), indicated by **S**.

THE OCTAVE

An **octave** is the range of **8 notes** of a major scale. The first note and last note of a major scale always have the same name. In the **C major** scale the distance from the lowest C to the C note above it is one octave (8 notes). The following example is one octave of the C major scale.

48 The C Major Scale

Each of the 8 notes in the major scale is given a **scale number**.

Note	C	D	E	F	G	A	B	C
Scale Number	1	2	3	4	5	6	7	8
Tone Pattern		T	T	ST	T	T	T	ST

T =Tone (2 frets)
ST =Semitone (1 fret)

The distance between two notes is called an **interval**.

In any major scale the interval between the 3rd to 4th note and the 7th to 8th note in the scale is one semitone (1 fret) apart. All other notes are one tone (2 frets) apart.

THE KEY OF C MAJOR

When a song consists of notes from a particular scale, it is said to be written in the **key** which has the same notes as that scale. For example, if a song contains mostly notes from the **C major scale**, it is said to be in the **key of C major**. The songs you have played in this book that commence with a C chord written above the first bar of music are in the key of C major.

The following two songs are in the key of C Major.

49 Jingle Bells

50 Michael Row the Boat Ashore

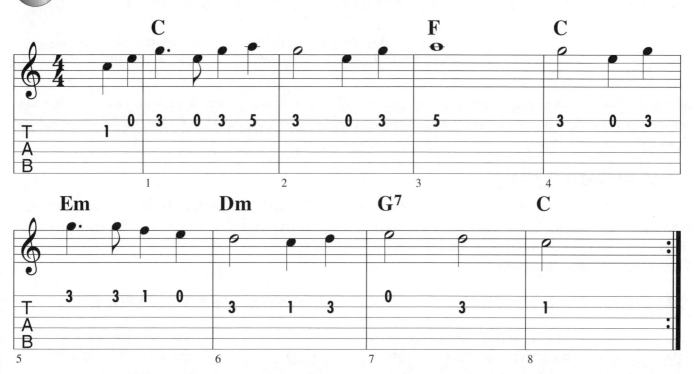

In any particular key, certain chords are more common than others, and after a while you will become familiar with the chords that belong to each key. Certain keys are easier for guitarists to play in and you should learn how to transpose (change the key of a song) so you can change a song that is in a difficult key (contains lots of sharps and flats or difficult chord shapes for a beginner to play) into an easier key.

The most common chords in the key of C major are;

C   Dm   Em   F   G7   Am

For more information on transposing and chords see *Progressive Guitar Method: Rhythm*.

LESSON TWELVE

THE G MAJOR SCALE

The **G major** scale starts and ends on the note G and contains an F sharp (**F♯**) note. Written below are two octaves of the **G major** scale. Notice that the **G major** scale has the same patterns of tones and semitones as the **C major** scale. In a major scale the interval between the 3rd to 4th note and the 7th to 8th notes is a semitone (1 fret). In the **G major** scale, to keep this pattern of tones and semitones correct, an F♯ note must be used instead of an F note.

 51 **The G Major Scale Over Two Octaves**

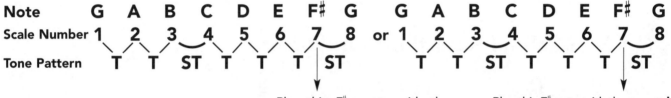

Songs in the key of C major use notes from the C major scale, songs in the key of G major use notes from the G major scale, so songs in the key of G major will contain F sharp (F♯) notes rather than F.

KEY SIGNATURES

Instead of writing a sharp sign before every F note on the staff, it is easier to write just one sharp sign after each clef. This means that all the F notes on the staff are played as F♯, even though there is no sharp sign written before them.
This is called a **key signature**.

C MAJOR KEY SIGNATURE

 The **C major** scale contains no sharps or flats, therefore the key signature for the key of **C major** contains no sharps or flats.

G MAJOR KEY SIGNATURE

 The **G major** scale contains one sharp, F♯, therefore the key signature for the key of **G major** contains one sharp, F♯.

The most common chords in the key of G major are;

G   Am   Bm   C   D7   Em

The following songs 'Minuet' and 'Lavenders Blue' are in the key of G major.
The key signature ⎣♯ tells you that all F notes on the music are played as F sharp (F♯).

These songs contain all the common chords in the key of G major.

LESSON THIRTEEN

THE F MAJOR SCALE

All major scales have the same pattern of tones and semitones, i.e. the interval between the 3rd and 4th note and the 7th to 8th note in the scale is a semitone (1 fret). For the F major scale to keep this pattern of tones and semitones a B flat (B♭) note must be used instead of a B note.

 54   The F Major Scale Over Two Octaves

Note	F	G	A	B♭	C	D	E	F		F	G	A	B♭	C	D	E	F
Scale Number	1	2	3	4	5	6	7	8	or	1	2	3	4	5	6	7	8
Tone Pattern		T	T	ST	T	T	T	ST			T	T	ST	T	T	T	ST

Songs in the key of F major use notes from the F major scale, so songs in the key of F major will contain B flat (B♭) notes rather than B.

F MAJOR KEY SIGNATURE

The **F major** scale contains one flat B♭, therefore the key signature for the key of **F major** contains one flat, B♭.

The most common chords in the key of F major are;

F   Gm   Am   B♭   C7   Dm

 55   The Galway Piper

56 Mary Ann

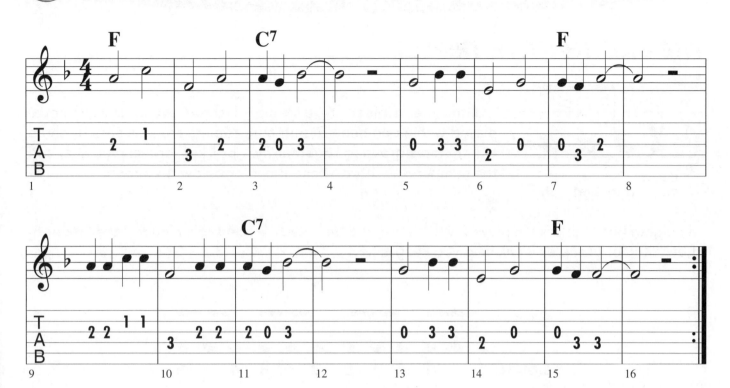

57 Billy Boy

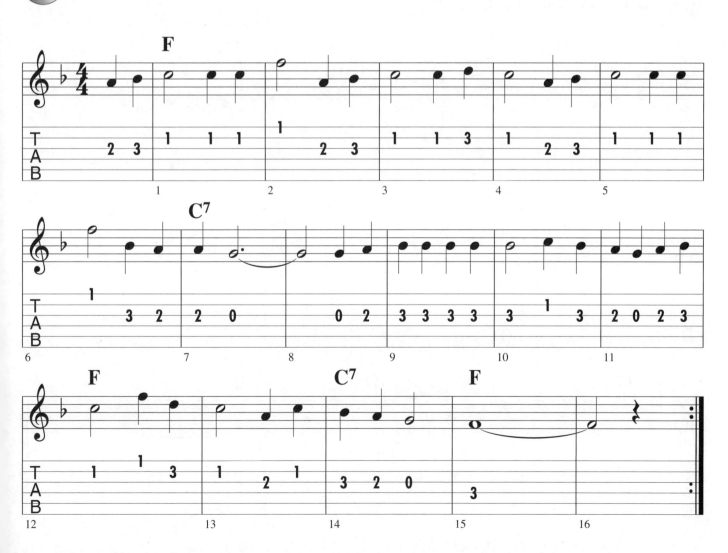

LESSON FOURTEEN

THE EIGHTH NOTE TRIPLET

Count: **1 + a**
Say: **one and ah**

Eighth note **triplets** are a group of **three** evenly spaced notes played within one beat. Eighth note triplets are indicated by three eighth notes grouped together by a bracket (or a curved line) and the number *3* written either above or below the group.

The eighth note triplets are played with a third of a beat each. **Accent** (play louder) the first note of each triplet group as it will help you keep time.

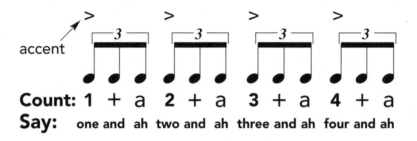

Count: **1 + a 2 + a 3 + a 4 + a**
Say: one and ah two and ah three and ah four and ah

58 Amazing Grace

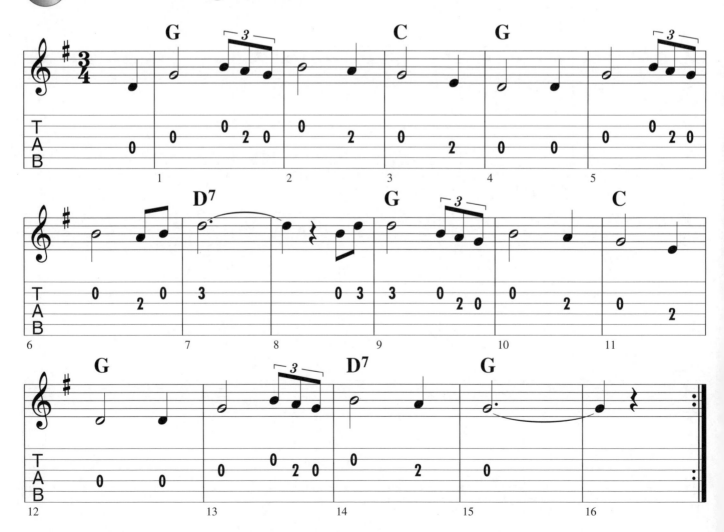

59 Beautiful Dreamer

SHUFFLE RHYTHM

The shuffle rhythm is a variation of triplet timing. It is created by not playing the middle note of the triplet group. In music notation the shuffle rhythm is indicated by an eighth rest replacing the middle note of the triplet.

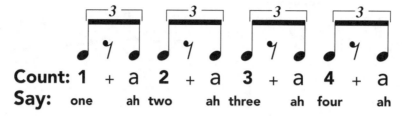

Count: **1** + a **2** + a **3** + a **4** + a
Say: one ah two ah three ah four ah

In the blues below the first beat of each bar is played as a shuffle rhythm with the remaining three beats of the bar played as eighth note triplets. To achieve the eighth rest place your left hand fingers lightly on the strings.

60 Shuffle Blues

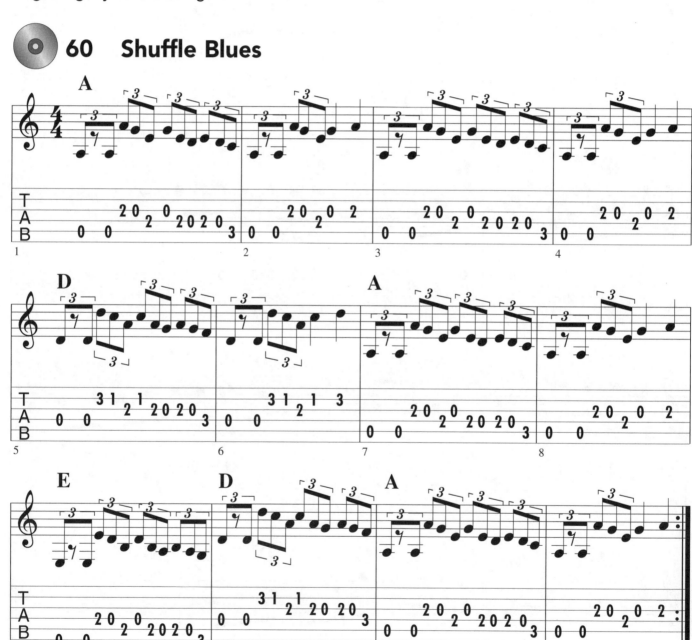

LESSON FIFTEEN

THE SIX EIGHT TIME SIGNATURE

 This is the **six eight** time signature.
There are six eighth notes in one bar of ⁶⁄₈ time. The six eighth notes are divided into two groups of three.

 or

Count: 1 2 3 4 5 6   1 2 3 4 5 6

When playing ⁶⁄₈ time there are **two** pulses within each bar with each beat being a **dotted quarter note.** (This is different to ⁴⁄₄ and ³⁄₄ time where each beat is a quarter note). **Accent** (play louder) the 1 and 4 count to help establish the two pulses per bar.

61 House of the Rising Sun

The songs 'House of the Rising Sun' and 'When Johnny Comes Marching Home' are in the key of A minor (Am). The notes used in these songs are from the A minor scale. The key signature for the key of A minor is the same as C major, i.e. it contains no sharps or flats.

C MAJOR KEY SIGNATURE   **A MINOR KEY SIGNATURE**

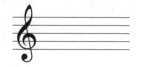   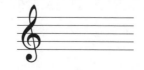

It is common for songs in the key of A minor to contain a G sharp (G♯) in its melody as in bar 14 of House of the Rising Sun. For more information on minor scales see *Progressive Guitar Method: Theory.*

62 When Johnny Comes Marching Home

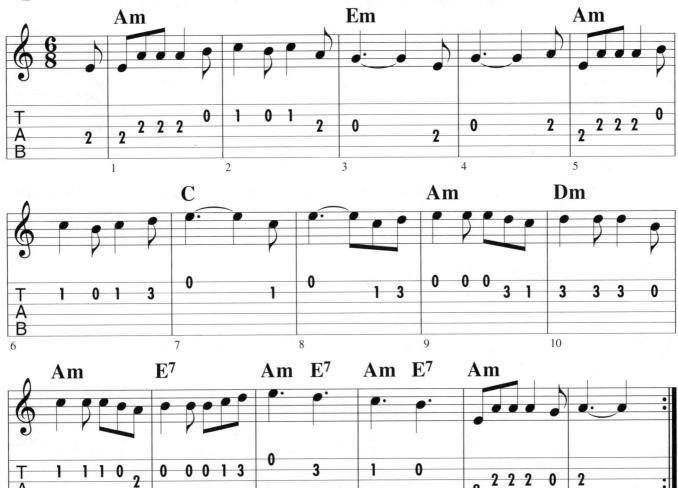

 63 The Irish Washerwoman

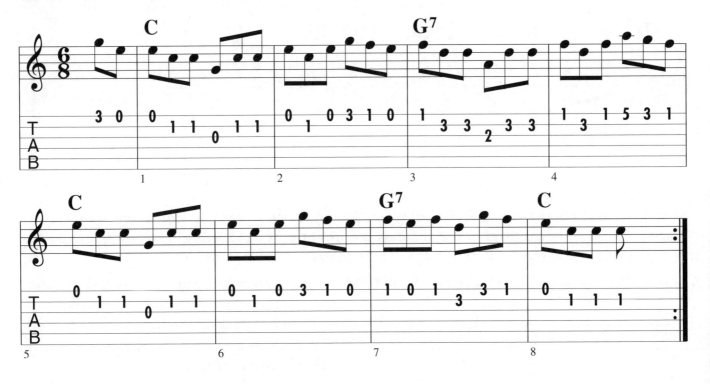

LESSON SIXTEEN

THE SIXTEENTH NOTE

 This is a **sixteenth note**.
It lasts for **one quarter** of a beat.
There are **four** sixteenth notes in one beat.
There are **16** sixteenth notes in one bar of $\frac{4}{4}$ time.

When sixteenth notes are played in conjunction with eighth notes the following timing combinations occur.

An easy way to remember these combinations is that they have the same timing as saying the words chucka-boom and boom-chucka.

Four sixteenth notes joined together.

Count: 1 e + a
Say: one 'ee' and 'ah'

Count: 1 e + a
Say: one 'ee' and
chucka - boom

Count: 1 e + a
Say: one and 'ah'
boom - chucka

64 Arkansas Traveller

DOTTED EIGHTH NOTES

Another common sixteenth note timing is when a sixteenth note is played after a dotted eighth note, i.e.

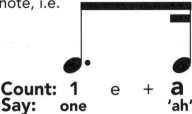

Count: 1   e   +   a
Say: one   'ah'

The dot placed after the eighth note lengthens the note by half its value. The dotted eighth note is equivalent to the duration of three sixteenth notes, i.e.

 65   El Condor Pasa

Another common key for guitar is the key of E minor (Em). El Condor Pasa is in the key of E minor and uses notes from the E minor scale. The key signature for E minor is the same as G major, i.e. it contains one sharp, F sharp (F♯). It is common for songs in the key of E minor to contain a D sharp (D♯) in the melody.

66 **Click Go the Shears**

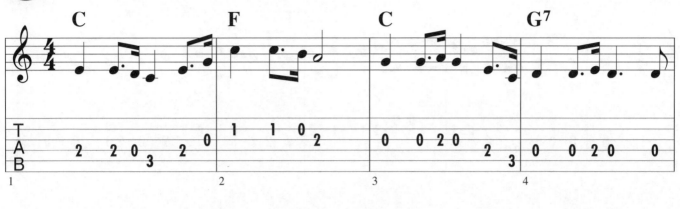

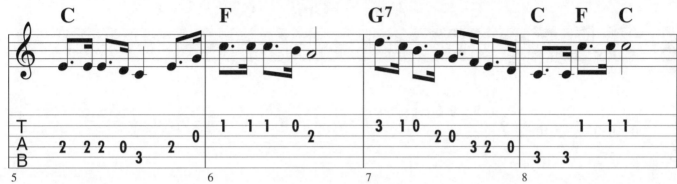

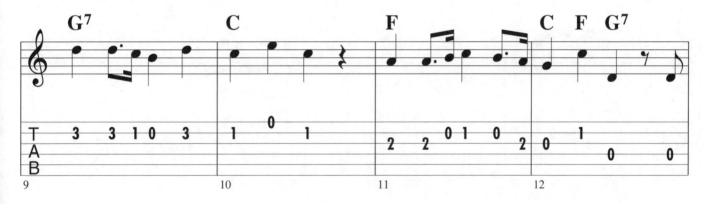

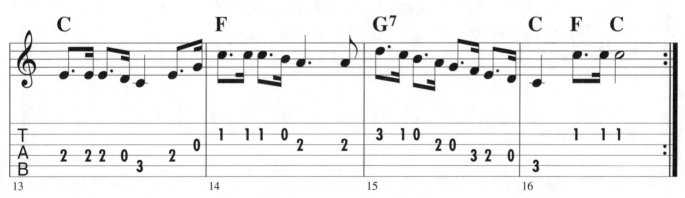

50

 67 **Battle Hymm of the Republic**

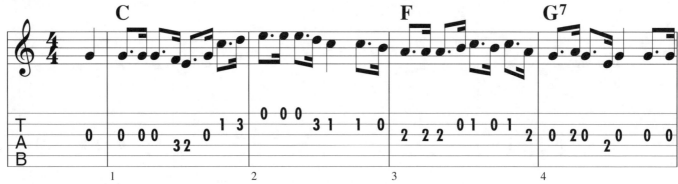

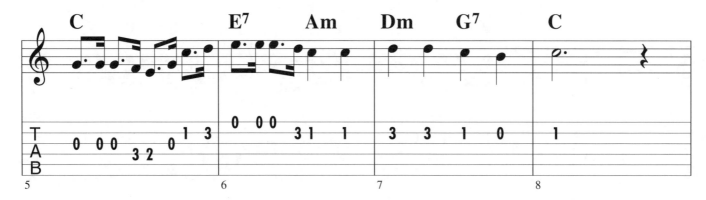

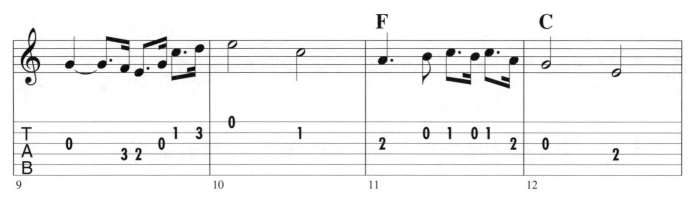

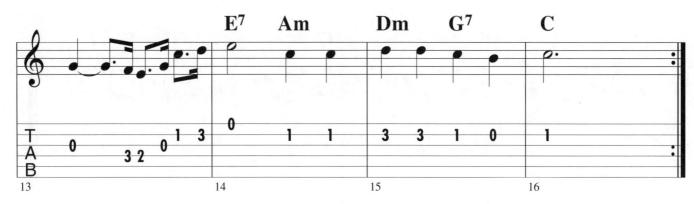

THE TWO FOUR TIME SIGNATURE

The $\frac{2}{4}$ time signature tells you that there are only two quarter note beats in one bar. The only difference between $\frac{2}{4}$ and $\frac{4}{4}$ is that in $\frac{2}{4}$ time there are twice as many bar lines.

68 Dixie

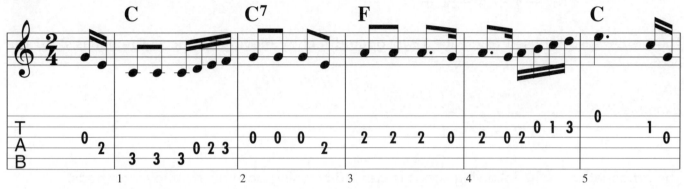

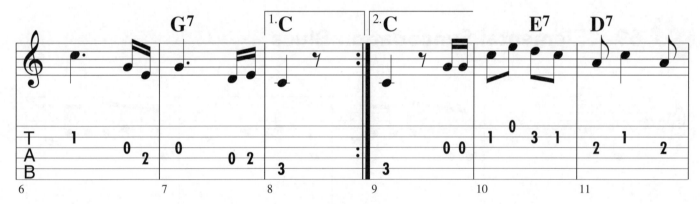

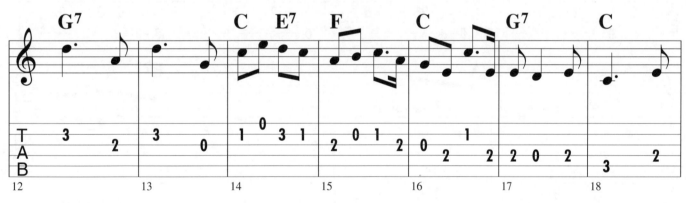

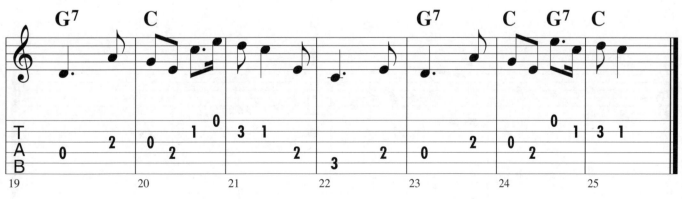

LESSON SEVENTEEN

SYNCOPATION

Syncopation occurs when notes are played "off" the beat, i.e. when notes are not played on the number part of the count but are played on the '+' part of the count.

Example 1

1 + 2 + 3 + 4 +

The tie can also be used to create a syncopated feel by moving the accent (emphasis) off the beat.

Example 2

1   2 + 3   4

The syncopation in the following songs is created by using both of the above methods.

69 **Elemental Syncopation Blues**

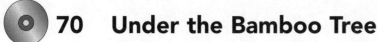

70 Under the Bamboo Tree

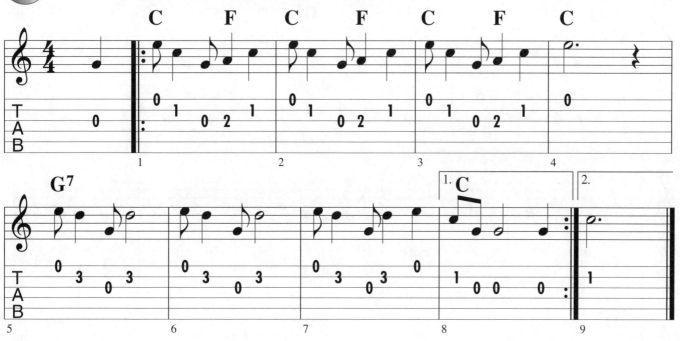

71 Jamaica Farewell

54

72   Tom Dooley

73   Sloop John B

74 Cottonfields

56

 75   The Entertainer

LESSON EIGHTEEN

SWING RHYTHMS

A swing rhythm is an eighth note triplet rhythm where the first and second notes of the triplet group are tied together;

Count: 1 + a

EIGHTH NOTE TRIPLETS

1 + a

SWING RHYTHM TIMING

1 + a

COMMON SWING RHYTHM NOTATION

To simplify the notation of a song using swing timing it is usual to write ♫ = ♩♪ at the top of the song. This indicates that although the music is written using eighth notes (♫) it is actually played using swing timing, i.e. ♩♪ The following songs use this notation.

76   Rhapsody in Blues

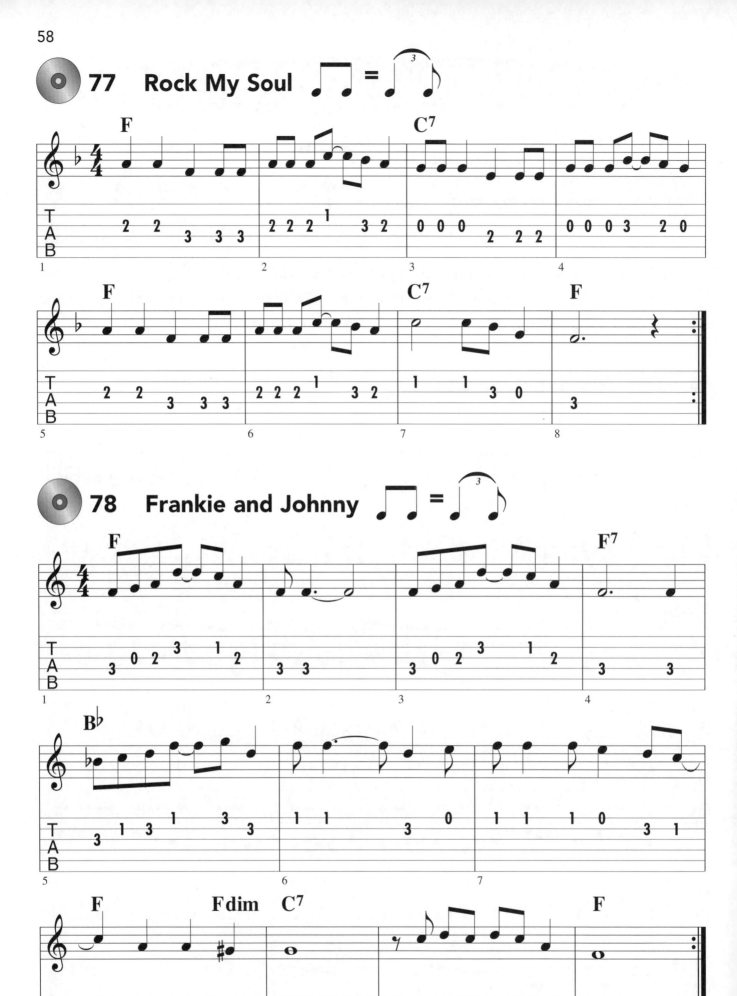

79 He's Got the Whole Wide World in His Hands

GLOSSARY OF MUSICAL TERMS

Accidental — a sign used to show a temporary change in pitch of a note (i.e. sharp ♯ , flat ♭ , double sharp ✖ , double flat ♭♭ , or natural ♮). The sharps or flats in a key signature are not regarded as accidentals.

Ad lib — to be played at the performer's own discretion.

Allegretto — moderately fast.

Allegro — fast and lively.

Andante — an easy walking pace.

Arpeggio — the playing of a chord in single note fashion.

Bar — a division of music occurring between two bar lines (also called a 'measure').

Bar chord — a chord played with one finger lying across all six strings on the guitar.

Bar line — a vertical line drawn across the staff dividing the music into equal sections called bars.

Bass — the lower regions of pitch in general. On guitar, the 4th, 5th and 6th strings.

Chord — a combination of three or more different notes played together.

Chord progression — a series of chords played as a musical unit (e.g. as in a song).

Clef — a sign placed at the beginning of each staff of music which fixes the location of a particular note on the staff, and hence the location of all other notes.

Coda — an ending section of music, signified by the sign ⊕ .

Common time — and indication of $\frac{4}{4}$ time — four quarter note beats per bar (also indicated by 𝐂).

D.C al fine — a repeat from the sign (indicated thus 𝄋) to the word 'fine'.

Dynamics — the varying degrees of softness (indicated by the term 'piano') and loudness (indicated by the term 'forte') in music.

Eighth note — a note with the value of half a beat in $\frac{4}{4}$ time, indicated thus ♪ (also called a quaver).

The eighth note rest — indicating half a beat of silence is written: ♭

Enharmonic — describes the difference in notation, but not in pitch, of two notes.

Fermata — a sign, ⌢ , used to indicate that a note or chord is held to the player's own discretion (also called a 'pause sign').

Flat — a sign, (♭)used to lower the pitch of a note by one semitone.

Forte — loud. Indicated by the sign 𝆑 .

Half note — a note with the value of two beats in $\frac{4}{4}$ time, indicated thus: ♩ (also called a minim). The half note rest, indicating two beats of silence, is written: ▬ on the third staff line.

Harmony — the simultaneous sounding of two or more different notes.

Interval — the distance between any two notes of different pitches.

Key — describes the notes used in a composition in regards to the major or minor scale from which they are taken; e.g. a piece 'in the key of C major' describes the melody, chords, etc., as predominantly consisting of the notes, **C, D, E, F, G, A,** and **B** — i.e. from the **C** scale.

Key signature — a sign, placed at the beginning of each stave of music, directly after the clef, to indicate the key of a piece. The sign consists of a certain number of sharps or flats, which represent the sharps or flats found in the scale of the piece's key.

Leger lines — small horizontal lines upon which notes are written when their pitch is either above or below the range of the staff.

Legato — smoothly, well connected.

Lick — a short musical phrase.

Major scale — a series of eight notes in alphabetical order based on the interval sequence tone - tone - semitone - tone - tone - tone - semitone, giving the familiar sound **do re mi fa so la ti do.**

Melody — a group of notes of varying pitch and duration, and having a recognizable musical shape.

Metronome — a device which indicates the number of beats per minute, and which can be adjusted in accordance to the desired tempo.

Moderato — at a moderate pace.**Natural** — a sign (♮)used to cancel out the effect of a sharp or flat. The word is also used to describe the notes **A, B, C, D, E, F** and **G**; e.g. 'the natural notes'.

Note — a single sound with a given pitch and duration.

Octave — the distance between any given note with a set frequency, and another note with exactly double that frequency. Both notes will have the same letter name.

Open voicing — a chord that has the notes spread out between both hands on the keyboard.

Pitch — the sound produced by a note, determined by the frequency of the string vibrations. The pitch relates to a note being referred to as 'high' or 'low'.

Plectrum — a small object (often of a triangular shape)made of plastic which is used to pick or strum the strings of a guitar.

Position — a term used to describe the location of the left hand on the guitar fret board. The left hand position is determined by the fret location of the first finger. The 1st position refers to the 1st to 4th frets. The 3rd position refers to the 3rd to 6th frets and so on.

Quarter note — a note with the value of one beat in $\frac{4}{4}$ time, indicated thus ♩ (also called a crotchet). The quarter note rest, indicating one beat of silence, is written: 𝄽 .

Repeat signs — used to indicate a repeat of a section of music, by means of two dots placed before a double bar line.

Rhythm — the note after which a chord or scale is named (also called 'key note').

Riff — a repeating pattern which may be altered to fit chord changes.

Semitone — the smallest interval used in conventional music. On guitar, it is a distance of one fret.

Sharp — a sign (♯) used to raise the pitch of a note by one semitone.

Staccato — to play short and detached. Indicated by a dot placed above the note.

Staff — five parallel lines together with four spaces, upon which music is written.

Syncopation — the placing of an accent on a normally unaccented beat.

Tempo — the speed of a piece.

Tie — a curved line joining two or more notes of the same pitch, where the second note(s) is not played, but its time value is added to that of the first note.

Timbre — a quality which distinguishes a note produced on one instrument from the same note produced on any other instrument (also called 'tone colour'). A given note on the guitar will sound different (and therefore distinguishable) from the same pitched note on piano, violin, flute etc. There is usually also a difference in timbre from one guitar to another.

Time signature — a sign at the beginning of a piece which indicates, by means of figures, the number of beats per bar (top figure), and the type of note receiving one beat (bottom figure).

Tone — a distance of two frets; i.e. the equivalent of two semitones.

Transposition — the process of changing music from one key to another.

Treble — the upper regions of pitch in general.

Treble clef — a sign placed at the beginning of the staff to fix the pitch of the notes placed on it. The treble clef (also called 'G clef') is placed so that the second line indicates as G note.

OTHER TITLES IN THE PROGRESSIVE SERIES

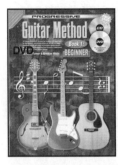

Guitar Method
Book 1

A comprehensive, lesson by lesson introduction to the guitar, covering notes on all 6 strings, reading music, picking technique, basic music theory and incorporating well known traditional pop/rock, folk and blues songs.

Guitar Method
Rhythm

Introduces all the important open chord shapes for major, minor, seventh, sixth, major seventh, minor seventh, suspended, diminished and augmented chords. Learn to play over 50 chord progressions, including 12 Bar Blues and Turnaround progressions.

Guitar Method
Lead

Covers scales and patterns over the entire fretboard so that you can improvise against major, minor, and Blues progressions in any key. Learn the licks and techniques used by all lead guitarists such as hammer-ons, slides, bending, vibrato, and more.

Guitar Method
Fingerpicking

Introduces right hand fingerpicking patterns that can be used as an accompaniment to any chord, chord progression or song. Covers alternate thumb, arpeggio and constant bass style as used in Rock, Pop, Folk, Country, Blues Ragtime and Classical music.

Guitar Method
Chords

Contains the most useful open, Bar and Jazz chord shapes of the most used chord types with chord progressions to practice and play along with. Includes sections on tuning, how to read sheet music, transposing, as well as an easy chord table, formula and symbol chart.

Guitar Method
Bar Chords

Introduces the most useful Bar, Rock and Jazz chord shapes used by all Rock/Pop/Country and Blues guitarist. Includes major, minor, seventh, sixth, major seventh, etc. Suggested rhythm patterns including percussive strums, dampening and others are also covered.

Guitar Method
Book 2

A comprehensive, lesson by lesson method covering the most important keys and scales for guitar, with special emphasis on bass note picking, bass note runs, hammer-ons etc. Featuring chordal arrangements of well known Rock, Blues, Folk and Traditional songs.

Guitar Method
Theory Book 1

A comprehensive, introduction to music theory as it applies to the guitar. Covers reading traditional music, rhythm notation and tablature, along with learning the notes on the fretboard, how to construct chords and scales, transposition, musical terms and playing in all keys.

PROGRESSIVE SCALES AND MODES FOR GUITAR
FOR BEGINNER TO ADVANCED

Progressive Scales and Modes gives the student a complete system for learning any scale, mode or chord and makes it easy to memorize any new new sound as well as building a solid visual and aural foundation of both the theory and the guitar fretboard. The book also shows you how to use each scale as well as how and why it fits with a particular chord or progression. The final section contains jam along progressions for every scale and mode presented in the book.

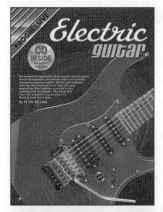

PROGRESSIVE ELECTRIC GUITAR
FOR BEGINNER TO INTERMEDIATE GUITARISTS
An innovative approach to learning the electric guitar which incorporates the volume and tone controls, the pickup selector switch, the tremolo arm, effects and amplifier settings into learning music from the very beginning. Explains and demonstrates all the essential chords, scales, rhythms and expressive techniques such as slides, bends, trills and vibrato. Also contains lessons on understanding the bass and drums and how to create parts which work with them. This book will have the student ready to play in a band in next to no time

PROGRESSIVE BLUES GUITAR
FOR BEGINNING BLUES GUITARISTS
A great introduction to the world of Blues Guitar. Covers all the essential rhythms used in Blues and R&B along with turnarounds, intros and endings, and gaining control of 12 and 8 bar Blues forms. Also explains and demonstrates the Blues scale, major and minor pentatonic scales and 7th arpeggios in a logical system for playing over the entire fretboard. Contains all the classic Blues sounds such as note bending, slides, and vibrato demonstrated in over 100 licks and solos in a variety of Blues styles.

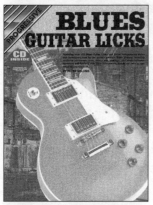

PROGRESSIVE BLUES GUITAR LICKS
FOR BEGINNER TO ADVANCED
Packed full of Blues guitar licks and solos incorporating styles and techniques used by the world's greatest Blues players. Includes sections on turnarounds, intro's and endings, call and response, dynamics and learning from other instruments. The licks cover a variety of styles such as shuffles, traditional slow Blues, Boogie, Jazz style Blues and R&B and Funk grooves. Also includes examples demonstrating how different licks can be put together to form whole solos, opening up endless possibilities for improvisation.

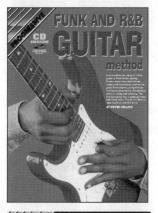

PROGRESSIVE FUNK AND R&B GUITAR METHOD
FOR BEGINNER TO ADVANCED
This book demonstrates many of the classic Funk sounds, using both rhythm and lead playing, since a good Funk player needs to be equally comfortable with both. A variety of chord forms are introduced within a framework that quickly allows the student to play confidently over the entire fretboard. Features an innovative approach to learning rhythms and applying them to riffs and grooves.

PROGRESSIVE JAZZ GUITAR
FOR BEGINNING JAZZ GUITARISTS
A lesson by lesson introduction to the most commonly used moveable chord shapes and progressions used by Jazz guitarists. Includes Jazz Blues progressions, turnarounds, chord construction and scale tone chords. All new chords are demonstrated with progressions to give a context for each sound. Also shows how to play in any key and how to transpose chords and progressions from one key to another.

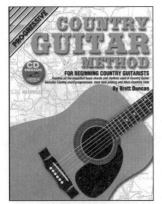

PROGRESSIVE COUNTRY GUITAR METHOD
FOR BEGINNER TO ADVANCED

Teaches the all important basic chords and rhythms used in Country Guitar by means of the two main classifications of Country guitar, rhythm and lead playing. Includes Country chord progressions, bass note picking and basic Country licks. There is also a special section dealing with tuning, the basics of music for Country guitar and an easy to read chord chart.

PROGRESSIVE CLASSICAL GUITAR METHOD
FOR BEGINNER TO ADVANCED

A comprehensive, lesson by lesson method covering all aspects of basic classical guitar technique such as proper hand techniques, progressing throught the most common keys and incorporating some of the world's most popular classical guitar pieces in solo or duet form. Music theory including the introduction of several different time signatures, open and bar chords and scales are also part of this easy to follow classical guitar method.

PROGRESSIVE LEAD GUITAR LICKS
FOR BEGINNER TO ADVANCED

Features over 110 licks incorporating the styles and techniques used by the world's best lead guitarists. Covers Rock, Blues, Metal, Country, Jazz, Funk, Soul, Rockabilly, Slide and Fingerpicking. Several solos are included to fully show how the licks and techniques can be used to create a lead guitar solo. The emphasis in this volume is to provide a vast variety of music styles to enable you to fit in with any music or recording situation. All licks are clearly notated using standard music notation and 'Easy Read' guitar tab.

PROGRESSIVE GUITAR CHORDS
FOR BEGINNER TO ADVANCED GUITARISTS

Shows you every useful chord shape in every key. An open chord section for beginners contains the simplest and most widely used chord shapes in all keys. A bar chord section for the semi-advanced player who will need a thorough knowledge of bar chord shapes in all positions. A section for the advanced player listing the moveable shapes for chords widely used by Jazz guitarists. Other sections contain important music theory for the guitarist including scales, keys and chord construction.

PROGRESSIVE BLUES RHYTHM GUITAR TECHNIQUE
FOR INTERMEDIATE BLUES GUITARISTS

Features great rhythm parts in a wide variety of Blues and R&B styles including shuffles, boogie, jump Blues, traditional slow Blues, Rock and Roll, Jazz and Funk. Shows you how to create rhythm parts using both chords and single note riffs and how to fit your parts to the style and instrumental combination you are playing with. Anyone who completes this book will be well on the way to being a great rhythm player.